Drawing and Sketching

Deri Robins

QED Publishing

First published in the UK in 2004 by
QED Publishing
A division of Quarto Publishing plc
The Fitzpatrick Building
188–194 York Way, London N7 9QP

A Catalogue record for this book is available
from the British Library.

ISBN 1 84538 045 2

Written by Deri Robins
Designed by Wladek Szechter/Louise Morley
Edited by Sian Morgan/Matthew Harvey
Illustrated by Melanie Grimshaw

Creative Director: Louise Morley
Editorial Manager: Jean Coppendale

Picture credits
Corbis Rune Hellestad p15
Jean Coppendale p26, p28

Printed and bound in China

The words in **bold** are
explained in the Glossary
on page 30.

Contents

Getting started   4

Get inspired!   6

Colour and shade   8

Self-portrait   10

Drawing faces   12

Drawing people   14

Moving figures   16

Perfect pets   18

Fur and feathers   20

Drawing a view   22

Looking at trees   24

Cityscapes   26

Using a grid   28

Glossary   30

Index   31

Notes for teachers   32

Getting started

Anyone can draw – it's just a matter of learning how to look! This book has lots of techniques to help you improve your drawings.

coloured pencils

To get started, you'll need some art kit. Start with a pad of paper, a couple of pencils and a pencil sharpener. As you learn more, you might want to try some of the materials below.

Pencils

You need at least three types of pencil: 2H (a hard pencil, for sharp lines and details); HB (medium hard, for sketching) and 2B (a soft pencil, for drawing guide lines and for **shading**). 4B to 8B pencils are very soft, and are for dark shading.

Eraser

Not just for rubbing out: you can use it to make **highlights** in your drawings by revealing the paper.

Charcoal and chalk

Charcoal and **chalk** are great for quick sketches, for large areas of colour and for adding **texture**.

Oil or chalk pastels

Chalk pastels are soft and crumbly, and give a delicate, blurry effect when you smudge them. Oil pastels make brighter colours.

Pens and felt tips

These are perfect for strong black lines or sharp detail. The **nibs** come in many different sizes – you need some thick and some thin ones.

Wax crayons

Cheap and good for making bold, colourful pictures and **resist work**.

Paper

Use lots of different types, sizes and colours of paper. You can make your own cheap sketchpads by simply stapling scrap paper together. Save your best paper for your final drawings. Experiment with paper with different surfaces: smooth **cartridge paper** is best for pencil and pen drawings. The rough surface of **sugar paper** is ideal for pastels, chalk, crayons and charcoal. The marks on the paper will look different depending on what sort of paper you use.

chalk

crayons

pastels

pencils

eraser

art paper

Get inspired!

You can get ideas for your drawing projects wherever you look. Carry a small sketchbook with you wherever you go so that you can jot down ideas and make quick, on-the-spot sketches. You can turn these into finished pictures later on.

When you find an interesting thing to draw, make a sketch and note its colour and **texture**. Texture is the surface of a thing – for example, it might be smooth, rough or bumpy.

Make an art collection

Collect interesting things to help you with your drawings. Create a mood-board of things that you like, such as leaves, coloured scraps of paper, patterns, photos, stamps, labels and pictures from newspapers and magazines. Paste them into a scrapbook or file them away neatly in a large box. You can use empty cereal boxes to make good art files.

Store your finished drawings safely in **portfolios**. You can make these from card or thick paper.

1 You'll need two large pieces of thick cardboard, a strip of material, some strong tape or glue and some string or ribbon.

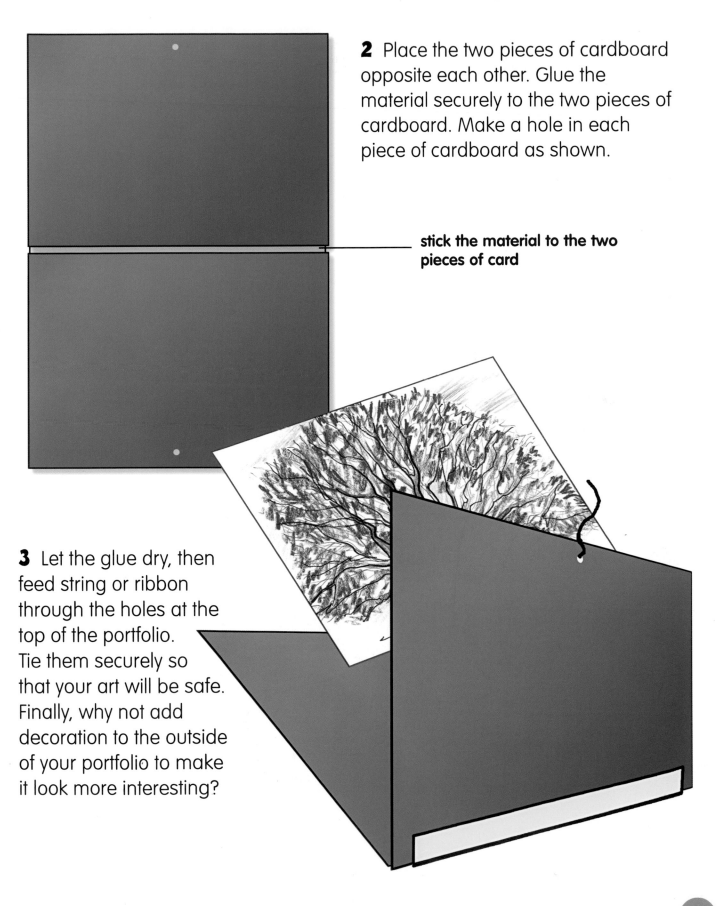

2 Place the two pieces of cardboard opposite each other. Glue the material securely to the two pieces of cardboard. Make a hole in each piece of cardboard as shown.

stick the material to the two pieces of card

3 Let the glue dry, then feed string or ribbon through the holes at the top of the portfolio. Tie them securely so that your art will be safe. Finally, why not add decoration to the outside of your portfolio to make it look more interesting?

Colour and shade

You can colour your drawing in solid blocks of colour – this makes bold, dramatic pictures, but it can look a bit flat. If you want your picture to look more three-dimensional, you need to add **shade**.

Hatching

This is how most artists add shade and **texture** to their drawings. You can make areas darker just by adding more lines. Try these techniques.

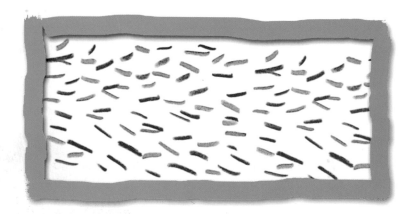

1 In cross-hatching, you draw two sets of lines running across each other.

2 Curved hatching lines are good for making shapes look round.

3 Use short lines for drawing fur or feathers. Experiment with pens and pencils.

4 The more lines you draw, the darker the shade.

Scribble shading

Small scribbles are good for fast, energetic-looking sketches, such as this one of a guinea pig.

Smudging

Smudging soft pencil, pastel or charcoal lines gives a soft shading effect.

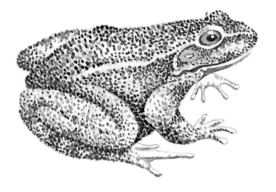

Making highlights

Use an eraser to rub bits of the shading out and make **highlights**. This can create pools of light or make parts of the picture look shiny.

Dot shading

Closely drawn dots give soft shade to a picture. Use more than one colour – look at them from a distance and they seem to blend together.

Self-portrait

One of the best ways to learn how to sketch people's faces is to draw pictures of yourself. First sketch a quick self-portrait from memory on scrap paper.

Perfect portraits

Is your face round, oval, heart-shaped, square or long? If you can't tell, use a soft pencil or crayon and trace the shape of your face on a mirror – then you can look at the outline and tell what shape it is.

Before you start your self-portrait, think about your features. What shape are your eyes? Are your lips thin or full? Is your nose long or short?

Follow the steps on page 11. Look carefully at your reflection and draw a picture of your face. Think about the **shading** and **texture**.

Compare it with the first sketch you did – you'll be amazed how much better your new drawing is!

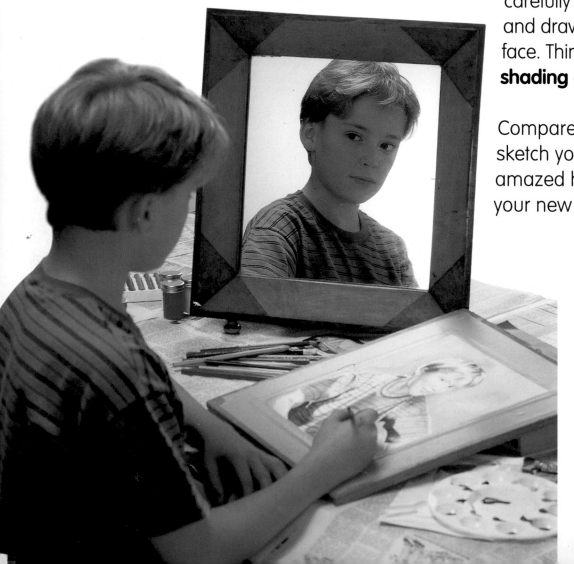

Start by looking carefully at yourself in the mirror. Think about where your ears are in relation to your eyes and nose.

Follow these steps to help you get all your features in the right place:

1 Use a soft pencil to sketch a faint egg shape for the **outline** of your face.

2 Draw a line down the middle of the face, and another one just above the centre from side to side.

3 Now divide the lower half into two. Then draw three more lines: one across and two up and down for the eyes.

4 Use the lines as a guide to sketch in your eyes. Leave one eye width between them. Draw your mouth: start with the line between the lips, then add the outline of the upper and lower lips. Draw in the tip of your nose, but not the sides.

5 Add your ears, hair, eyelashes, eyebrows, chin and other details. Now you can add shading and colour with coloured pencils.

Drawing faces

Once you feel confident about drawing yourself, try drawing other people. Faces come in all shapes and sizes, and everyone's features are different. You can build up hundreds of different faces by making an Identikit set.

Identikit set

1 Draw four or five different face shapes, and divide them into sections.

2 Now cut lots of strips of paper, each the same width as the sections in the face.

3 Draw different-shaped eyes on some of the strips, noses on others and mouths on the rest, all with different expressions.

4 Now mix and match the features on the different faces. You can cut out hairlines, moustaches and glasses, too.

5 When you've created a face you like, trace or copy the **outline** and features onto another piece of paper. Use coloured pencils to turn it into a finished drawing.

EGG HEADS

It's not quite so easy to draw people's faces from the side, or from above or below! A hard-boiled egg can be a very useful part of your art kit.

1 Draw lines on the egg exactly as shown.

2 Draw in the features. Stick a blob of Plasticine on for the nose.

3 Using your egg-head as a model, practise drawing faces from different angles.

ART FILE

People don't smile all the time! Collect photos and newspaper cuttings of faces with different expressions, and practise drawing them.

Drawing people

The easiest way to draw figures is to think about the parts of the body as simple shapes. For example, think of the head as an egg, and the arms and legs as sausages!

1 Start with the head at the top of your paper. Draw an egg shape.

2 Add a short tube for the neck. It should be almost as wide as the head.

3 Now draw an egg shape for the top of the body.

4 Draw the arms as if they were two sausage shapes joined in the middle.

5 Draw the rest of the body using egg shapes and circles.

6 Draw the legs in the same way as the arms, but make them wider at the top.

7 Finally, add simple hand and feet shapes and draw the final **outline** to your figure.

Now draw your sausage and egg figures sitting, lying or crawling. Look at people in different poses or from different angles to get some ideas.

TRY THIS

If you draw these shapes roughly first of all, you can add the details later. Sketch lightly with a soft pencil. Rub out the original lines when your drawing is complete.

Make a poster

Find some photos of your favourite sports, movie or pop star, and draw him or her by building up from simple shapes.

Use different pens, pencils and crayons for your picture. What different effects can you create? Remember to use **shading** for the dark areas and leave **highlights** for the light areas.

FOOTBALL

Moving figures

How can you make figures look as if they are really moving? A number of simple techniques will help you bring your sketches to life.

Art in action

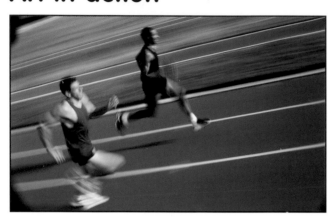

Choose a photograph of someone moving. Make a quick sketch of the figure, using loose strokes. Use your whole arm and not just your fingers and wrists. Try to look at the figure – not at what you are drawing!

Keep your pencil moving all the time, hardly lifting it from the paper. Draw sweeping lines that follow the direction of the motion. This will help convey the illusion of speed and movement, and make your figure look more realistic.

TIP

Take your sketchbook to an event where there will be lots of movement, for example football, ice skating, gymnastics or dance. Make speedy sketches of the figures. You could also video an event from television. Freeze-frame the moments you are trying to capture.

Practise drawing action shots of sports people or dancers. The trick is not to draw detailed pictures of the people, just what they are doing.

Try using coloured pencils to make bold scribble drawings.

Finally, use your sketches to help you draw a finished picture.

TIP

Adding 'speed lines' really brings your action figures to life! Curved lines make your figures look as if they are twirling around. Straight lines make your figures look as if they are flashing past!

Perfect pets

Just as human figures can be made up of 'eggs and sausages' (page 14), you can draw great pictures of pets by combining simple shapes.

Cat

You can draw a cat from three simple circles.

1 Using a soft pencil, lightly sketch three circles, two for the body and one for the head. Make the head smaller than the body. Add the ears, front legs and the curl of the tail.

2 Use coloured pencils to complete the **outline** of the cat. You can now rub out any lines that you don't need.

3 Add details, such as eyes, whiskers, fur and markings.

1

2

3

Here are some other animals for you to sketch.

Collect pictures of as many animals as you can find. Save photos of your pets or of a pet that you would like to have. Collect pictures of your favourite animals on stamps, greetings cards, magazines or websites.

TIP

Try drawing different types of cats and dogs from photos – or from life, if they will sit still long enough! Remember that heads, tails, ears and fur are never the same, so look at them carefully before you begin.

Fur and feathers

Sketching the **outline** is the first step when drawing animals. To really bring your drawings to life, you need to add **texture**. One way to do this is to make different types of markings with coloured pencils.

Dogs and cats

Use soft pencils to scribble a curly coat, or to draw a fluffy tail.

Reptiles

Snakes, lizards and tortoises have interesting **geometric** patterns and markings.

Fish

Lots of little curved lines are ideal for the scales of a fish.

Birds

Use long, straight lines for the tail feathers, and short, curvy lines for head and chest. Hard pencils are good for drawing feathers.

Experiment with different art materials to see which ones produce the most realistic effects for your animals.

Try drawing the same animal using different materials. What happens? How are they different?

Soft pencils or charcoal give a wider, softer effect, and are perfect for drawing fluffy animals.

What happens if you use pastels, chalks and crayons?

Hard pencils make thin, light lines – great for showing up this squirrel's fluffy tail.

Pens and felt tips make strong, black lines – the finer the point, the thinner the lines.

Drawing a view

When it comes to drawing a view, how do you decide which bits to put in, and which to leave out? Making a viewfinder can help you to decide.

Make a viewfinder

A viewfinder is a piece of card with a hole in the middle. If you make it out of two L-shaped pieces of card clipped together, you can change the shape to make a square or a rectangle.

1 Cut an L-shape out of card. Trace around it to make an identical shape, and cut this out too.

2 Use paperclips to hold the pieces together and make a rectangle.

1

2

TIP

Silver or white pencils look good on black **sugar paper**. Use black pens or thick felt tips to draw **silhouettes** – such as a winter **landscape** or a sunset. Silhouettes are solid dark **outlines** on a lighter **background**. They look good against soft white tissue paper or silver backgrounds.

1

Using the viewfinder

1 Hold the viewfinder in front of you. Look through the hole in the middle as if it were a camera lens. Move it around until you find the right view. What happens when you look at the same view **horizontally** and **vertically**?

2 When you have chosen your view, with one hand, quickly sketch the main parts of the picture with a soft pencil (you can rub it out afterwards). This is your rough outline for the finished picture to indicate large areas, such as grass, sky or water. Sketch in the position of any buildings or trees.

3 When you have done the outlines, put the viewfinder away and finish the picture, putting in the details and using coloured pencils, chalks or pastels.

2

3

Looking at trees

As with all your drawings, it is important to look carefully at a tree before you try to draw it. Notice how the branches grow from one another, rather than all coming straight from the trunk.

There are a huge variety of tree shapes.

Some trees have long branches that reach out to the side.

Some trees are are very tall and thin.

UP CLOSE

Bark varies enormously, too. Rubbings are a great way to collect different types of bark for reference. Put a piece of white paper over a section of the trunk and rub the surface with a soft pencil or crayon.

It can help to sketch the overall shape of a tree before you draw in the detail.
Try filling the whole piece of paper with your tree shape to make it really dramatic.

1 Lightly sketch in the trunk and the overall **outline** of the tree.

2 Draw the main branches, making them thinner at the ends.

3 Add fine lines for the smaller twigs, right up to the edge of the outline.

This is how the tree looks in winter, but deciduous trees change throughout the year. Leaves appear, change colour and fall; buds can be followed by blossom and then berries.

Soft pencils or charcoal are ideal for drawing wintry trees. For a dramatic effect, use white chalk on black paper. Just colour the spaces around the tree, and in between the branches, to make dramatic **silhouettes**.

Cityscapes

A cityscape is a view of a city. Don't be put off by thinking that buildings are too complicated – the trick is to look at everything carefully and to build up the picture from patterns and shapes.

1 Decide what you are going to put into your picture. Are there any interesting buildings in your area? Use your viewfinder to help you decide which is the best view. You could use a view on a postcard or from a book.

2 Firstly, draw the **outlines** on a wide piece of paper. Look carefully at the buildings – are they wider than they are tall? Do the roofs slope steeply or are they shallow?

3 When you have done the outlines, sketch in the doors and windows. Check how big they are compared with the rest of the building.

4 Add the rest of the details, such as chimneys, turrets, porches, steps, stones, wood and brick patterns. Finish by adding colour, using white to create **highlights** for bright spots.

Build your own

To make a building look three-dimensional, you need to draw its side view as well as its front.

1 Draw the front of the building.

2 Draw in the sides, to make a **cube**.

3 Add a roof, door and windows.

4 Shade the side of the house lightly – you could add a shadow to make it look realistic.

Using a grid

Drawing is about looking and copying exactly what you see. Sometimes our mind tricks us and we draw what we expect to see, not what is actually in front of us. Using a grid can help you get the **proportions** exactly right and can also help you to make your pictures larger or smaller.

1 Take a photo or magazine cutting, and trace the **outline** of the picture you want to copy onto tracing paper. Now divide your tracing into equal squares, using a ruler to help you.

2 Take a sheet of paper, and make the same number of squares, using a soft pencil. You can make the squares the same size as the ones on the tracing paper, or they can be smaller or bigger.

3 Copy the main outlines of the picture into each square one by one. Concentrate on each square at a time, rather than looking at the whole picture.

Upside-down drawing

Choose a picture from a magazine that you'd like to draw, and rule it into squares. Make a separate grid on a sheet of white paper. Turn the original picture upside down. Now copy each square, including all the **shading**. Your finished picture will be much more accurate, because you are just copying areas of colour and shade, rather than trying to draw the details.

Using a piece of wallpaper lining, make a big poster of an animal for your wall. Use the grid technique with chalks or charcoals to fill in large areas quickly.

4 When the main outline is complete, rub out the guidelines and fill in the smaller details, using the photo as a guide.

Glossary

background
the area of a picture behind the main object – for example, a field and distant hills

cartridge paper
very smooth, high-quality paper – good for finished drawings

chalk
a soft stick of rock used for making soft, smudgy pictures

charcoal
a drawing tool made from charred wood

cube
a square, six-sided, 3-D shape

geometric
made from a regular pattern

highlights
the bright parts of a picture

horizontal
horizontal lines run across the page

landscape
a scene – eg. a country landscape, showing trees and hills, or an industrial landscape, showing factories and buildings

nib
the writing end of a pen

outline
the outer lines of your picture – usually you draw these first and add the details later

portfolio
a case for storing and carrying your drawings

proportion
the relative size of one thing to another

resist work
a form of printing in which you cover a raised surface with ink or paint and then press this down on a sheet of paper

shading
colouring part of your drawing in to make it darker

silhouette
a solid picture that is done by drawing an outline and filling it in

sugar paper
a rough-textured paper – good for chalk and charcoal drawings

texture
the surface of something – some paper has smooth texture, others have a rougher texture

vertical
vertical lines run from top to the bottom

Index

action shots 16–17
animals 18–19
    fur and feathers 8,
    20–21
art collection 6

background 22, 30
bark rubbings 24
buildings 23, 26–27

cartridge paper 4, 30
chalk 4, 5, 23, 25, 30
chalk pastels 4
charcoal 4, 5, 9, 21, 25,
    30
circles 18
cityscapes 26–27
colour 8
crayons 4, 5, 15, 21, 24
cross-hatching 8
cubes 27, 30

dot shading 9

egg shapes 11, 13, 14, 15
eraser 4, 5, 9
expressions 13

faces 10–11
    from different angles
    13
    Identikit 12–13
feathers 8, 20, 21
features 12–13
felt tips 4, 21, 22
figures 14–15, 16–17
files 6

fur 8, 20–21
geometric patterns 20,
    30
grid 28–29

hatching 8
highlights 4, 9, 15, 26, 30
horizontal 23, 30

ideas 6
Identikit faces 12–13
inspiration 6

landscape 22, 30
lines, showing
    movement 16–17

materials 4–5
mood board 6
movement 16–17

nibs 4, 30

oil pastels 4
outlines 10, 14, 18, 20, 22,
    25, 26, 28, 30

paper 4–5
pastels 4, 9, 23
pencils 4, 9, 20, 21, 23,
    25
pens 4, 21, 22
people 14–15
    faces 10–13
    movement 16–17
pets 18–19
photos 13, 16, 19, 29

portfolio 6–7, 30
portraits 10–11
posters 15, 29
proportions 28, 30

resist work 4, 30

scrapbook 6, 19
scribble drawings 17
scribble shading 9
self-portrait 10–11
shading 4, 8–9, 10–11, 15,
    27, 29, 30
shadows 27
silhouettes 22, 25, 30
sketchbook 16
sketches 6, 16
sketchpads 4
smudging 4, 9
speed lines 17
sugar paper 5, 22, 30

texture 4, 6, 8, 10, 20, 30
three-dimensional effects
    8, 27, 30
trees 23, 24–25

upside-down drawing 29

vertical 23, 30
vertical views 23
videos 16
viewfinder 22–23, 26
views 22–23

wax crayons 4

Notes for teachers

The projects in this book are aimed at Key Stage 2 children. You can use them as stand-alone lessons, or as a part of other topics or subjects. The ideas in the book offer children inspiration, but you should always encourage them to draw from their own imagination and first-hand observation as well as from memory.

Sourcing ideas

All art projects should tap into children's interests, and be relevant to their lives and experiences. Some stimulating starting points might be: found objects, discussions about their family and pets, hobbies, TV programmes or topical events.

Encourage children to source their own ideas and references, from books, magazines, the Internet or CD-ROMs. Digital cameras can create reference material (pictures of landscapes, people or animals) that can be used alongside children's finished work (see below).

Other lessons can often be an ideal springboard for an art project – for example, a geography field trip can lead to a collection of bark rubbings and leaves, which would make a bank of ideas for a landscape picture.

Encourage children to keep a sketchbook of their ideas, and to collect other images and objects to help them develop their drawings.

Give pupils as many first-hand experiences as possible through visits and contact with creative people.

Evaluating work

It's important and motivating for children to share their work with others, and to compare ideas and methods. Encourage them to talk about their work. What do they like best about it? How would they do it differently next time?

Show the children examples of other artists' work – how did they tackle the same subject and problems? Do the children like the work? Why? Why not?

Help children to judge the originality and value of their work, to appreciate the different qualities in others' work and to value ways of working that are different from their own. Display all the children's work.

Going further

Look at ways to develop projects – for example, many of the ideas in this book could be adapted into painting, collage and print-making. You could use image-enhancing computer software and digital scanners to build up and juxtapose images.

Show the children how to set up a class art gallery on the school website. Having their work displayed professionally will make them feel that their work is valued.